To help people understand what God is like,
Jesus told lots of stories which are as exciting
today as when they were first heard.

The Ten Silver Coins is still a great favourite
and its message is one that children especially
love to hear.

This edition published by Candle Books in 2008,
a publishing imprint of Lion Hudson plc.

Distributed in the UK by Marston Book Services Ltd,
PO Box 269, Abingdon, Oxon OX14 4YN

Scripture quotations in this book are taken from the Good News Bible © 1966, 1971,
1976, 1992 American Bible Society.

International publishing rights owned by Zondervan®.
Worldwide co-edition produced by Lion Hudson plc,
Wilkinson House, Jordan Hill Road, Oxford, OX2 8DR
Tel: +44 (0)1865 302750 Fax: +44 (0)1865 302757
Email: coed@lionhudson.com www.lionhudson.com

ISBN 978 1 85985 750 2

Printed in China

NICK BU—————————INKPEN

THE TEN SILVER COINS

CANDLE BOOKS

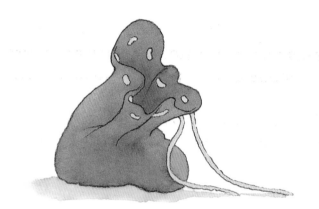

NICK BUTTERWORTH AND MICK INKPEN

THE TEN SILVER COINS

Here is a woman. She has ten silver coins. She likes to count them.

One, two, three, four . . .

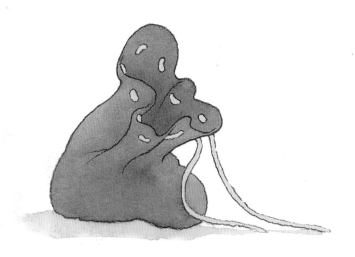

Oops! Silly cat! Now they've
gone all over the place.

The woman picks up her
silver coins. They have been
scattered everywhere!

The cat doesn't care. He has
stretched out and gone
to sleep.

The woman counts her silver coins again. But there are only nine. Bother! One of them is missing.

Never mind, it can't have gone far.

Perhaps it is under the rug.
No. There is no sign of it there.

Perhaps it has bounced into the fireplace. Carefully she sifts through the ashes.

What a messy job! But no, there is no coin.

Perhaps it rolled right under the door and out into the garden.

She searches and searches, but she cannot find the coin anywhere.

She even looks inside her
pots and pans, even though she
really knows it can't be there.

Clatter! Bang! What a noise
she is making!

She's making so much noise, she's woken up the cat. Serves him right. He's off to find a quiet spot in the garden.

There it is! The cat was lying on it all the time! The missing silver coin is found!

The woman laughs. She is so
happy she calls a friend to
tell her the good news.

Jesus says, 'We are like the woman's silver coins. God wants every single one of us.'

*Jesus said, 'Or suppose a woman who has ten silver coins loses
one of them – what does she do?
She lights a lamp, sweeps her house, and looks carefully
everywhere until she finds it. When she finds it, she calls her
friends and neighbours together, and says to them,
"I am so happy I found the coin I lost. Let us celebrate!"
In the same way, I tell you, the angels of God rejoice
over one sinner who repents.'*

Luke 15:8–10

Other titles from **Candle Books** *by*
Nick Butterworth and Mick Inkpen

The House On The Rock
The Lost Sheep
The Precious Pearl
The Good Stranger
The Two Sons
The Rich Farmer
The Ten Silver Coins
The Little Gate

Stories Jesus Told
Animal Tales
Stories Jesus Told Colouring Book